The Night

One evening, Yok-Yok watches the sun slowly going down.

On this night, the sun comes down in front of the
mountains.

And it goes to sleep in Yok-Yok's nutshell.

Yok-Yok looks at the stars that shine in the night.

With a large butterfly net, he catches some of them.

Yok-Yok puts them in his nutshell. Now he can sleep
with the sun and the stars.

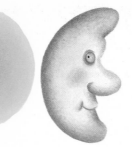

During the day
the sun gives light and warmth to the earth.
At night, you can see
the moon and the stars in the sky.
The stars are usually bigger than the earth.
But they seem quite small
because they are very far away.

The Breakfast Visitor

Someone is getting the table ready for breakfast.

And look who's in the sugar bowl! It's Yok-Yok!

Yok-Yok has a sweet tooth. He climbs out of the
sugar bowl with a lump of sugar. Then he dips it
in the good hot chocolate.

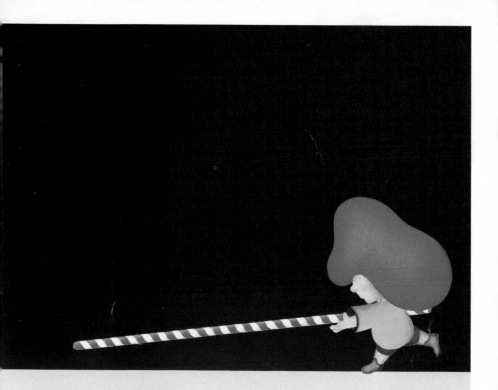

But what's Yok-Yok doing now?

With a straw for a pole, he bounces like a champion jumper onto a carton of milk.

'Mmmm! The milk is good!"

Eggs are often eaten for breakfast.
They can be hard-boiled or soft-boiled,
fried, scrambled, or poached.
A good breakfast often includes eggs,
as well as milk,
bread, fruit or juice,
and a hot drink.

The Ladybugs

Yok-Yok takes a beautiful red ladybug in his hands
and counts the black spots on its back.

"I can play dominoes," thinks Yok-Yok. "I can put five spots beside five spots..."

"And I can put two spots beside two spots..."

But one of the ladybugs does not want to play anymore.
It goes away.

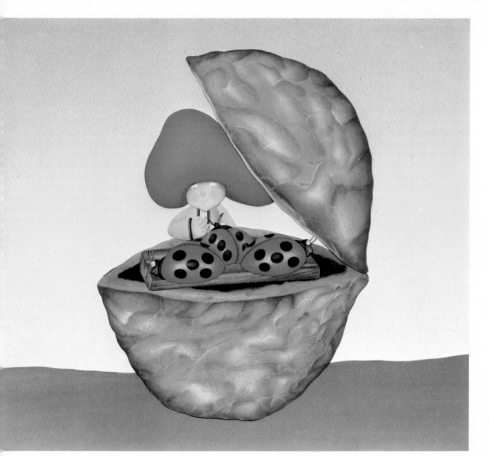

Yok-Yok catches it again and puts it back into
his nutshell.

But the ladybug will not stay where he puts it.
"Well, go if you must," says Yok-Yok.
"We'll play a different game."

A ladybug is also called a ladybird.
It is a small beetle.
Most kinds of ladybugs are welcome in gardens,
because they eat insects that harm plants.
It is thought to be bad luck
to harm a ladybug.
And it is thought to be a sign of good luck
when a ladybug is on a person
and leaves unharmed.

The Bird in the Nest

"Hello, bird!" says Yok-Yok.

And he slides into the nest.

Yok-Yok feels very warm under the wings of his friend the bird.

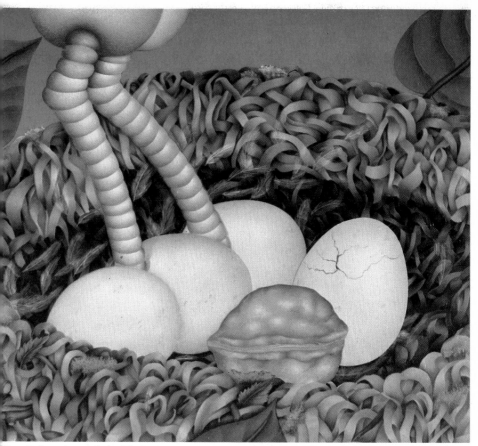

Suddenly, Yok-Yok hears a tiny crackling sound.

A little bird covered with soft downy feathers, comes out of one of the eggs. "It must be hungry," thinks Yok-Yok.

He reaches into his nutshell. "Here, bird,"
says Yok-Yok. "Eat this raspberry."
And the baby bird opens its large beak.

A bird chooses a place
that is well sheltered for its home.
With a lot of care and patience, it builds its nest.
It uses things like twigs, moss,
dry grass, animal fur, and mud.
A bird lays its eggs in the nest.
Then it sits on the eggs to keep them warm
until the baby birds hatch.